Discovering Your
Spiritual Gifts

Other Women of Faith Bible Studies

WOMEN OF FAITH℠
BIBLE STUDY SERIES

Discovering Your
Spiritual Gifts

Written by
PHYLLIS BENNETT

General Editor
TRACI MULLINS

ZondervanPublishingHouse
Grand Rapids, Michigan

A Division of HarperCollins*Publishers*

Discovering Your Spiritual Gifts
Copyright © 1998 by Women of Faith, Inc.

Requests for information should be addressed to:

ZondervanPublishingHouse
Grand Rapids, Michigan 49530

ISBN: 0-310-21340-1

General Editor, Traci Mullins
Cover and interior illustration by Jim Dryden
Interior design by Sue Vandenberg Koppenol

Printed in the United States of America

98 99 00 01 02 03 04 /❖ EP/ 10 9 8 7 6 5 4 3 2 1

CONTENTS

FOREWORD

The best advice I ever received was in 1955. I was twenty-three. Somebody had the good sense to say to me, "Luci, if you want to give yourself a gift, learn all you can about the Bible. Start going to a Bible class and don't stop until you have some knowledge under your belt. You won't be sorry." Having just graduated from college, I was living with my parents, and together we drove more than twenty miles to attend that class. We went four nights a week for two years. I've *never* been sorry.

Nothing I've ever done or learned has meant more to me than those classes. Unless I was on my deathbed, I didn't miss. I went faithfully, took notes, absorbed everything like a sponge, asked questions relentlessly, and loved *every* minute! (I probably drove the teacher crazy.)

Today, more than forty years later, this wonderful storehouse of truth is my standard for living, giving, loving, and learning. It is my Rock and Fortress, the pattern for enjoying abundant life on earth, and for all eternity. I know what I believe, and why. I'm open to change on my tastes, personal opinions, even some of my choices. But change my biblical convictions? No way! They're solid and secure, based on God's inerrant, enduring, and unchanging Word. There's nothing like learning God's truth. As he says, it sets you free.

Women of Faith Bible studies are designed to help you deal with everyday problems and issues concerning you. Experienced and wise women who, like the rest of us, want to know God intimately, have written these lessons. They encourage us to dig into the Scriptures, read them carefully, and respond to thought-provoking questions. We're invited to memorize certain verses as sources of support and guidance, to hide his Word in our heads and hearts.

The clever ideas in these studies make me smile. The stories move my spirit. There are valuable suggestions in dealing with others, quotations that cause me to stop and think. The purpose of every activity is to put "some knowledge under your belt" about the Bible and its relevance for life *this very day.*

Give yourself a gift. Grab your Bible, a pencil, notepad, cup of coffee . . . maybe even a friend . . . and get started. I assure you—you'll *never* be sorry.

LUCI SWINDOLL

HOW TO USE THIS GUIDE

Women of Faith Bible studies are designed to take you on a journey toward a more intimate relationship with Christ by bringing you together with your sisters in the faith. We all want to continue to grow in our Christian lives, to please God, to be a vital part of our families, churches, and communities. But too many of us have tried to grow alone. We haven't found enough places where we feel safe to share our heartaches and joys and hopes. We haven't known how to support and be supported by other women in ways that really make a difference. Perhaps we haven't had the tools.

The guide you are about to use will give you the tools you need to explore a fundamental aspect of your walk with God *with* other women who want to grow, too. You'll not only delve into Scripture and consider its relevance to your everyday life, but you'll also get to know other women's questions, struggles, and victories—many similar, some quite different from your own. This guide will give you permission to be yourself, to share honestly, to care for one another's wounds, and laugh together when you take yourselves too seriously.

Each of the six lessons in this guide is divided into six sections. Most you'll discuss as a group; others you'll cover on your own during the week between meetings.

A Moment for Quiet Reflection. The questions in this section are meant to be answered in a few minutes of privacy sometime before you join your group each week. You may already carve out a regular time of personal reflection in your days, so you've experienced the refreshment and insight these times bring to your soul. However, if words like "quiet," "reflection," and "refreshment" have become unfamiliar to you, let this guide get you started with the invaluable practice of setting aside personal time to think, to rest, to pray. Sometimes the answers you write down to the questions in this section will be discussed as a group when you come together; other times they'll just give you something to ponder deep within. Don't neglect this important reflection time each week, and include enough time to read the introduction to the lesson so you'll be familiar with its focus.

Knowing God's Heart. The questions in this section will take you into the Bible, where you and the women in your group can discover God's heart and mind on the subject at hand. You'll do the Bible study together, reading the Scriptures aloud and sharing your understanding of the passage so all of you can learn together what God has to say about your own heart and life, right now. While you don't need to complete the study questions prior to each group session, it will be helpful for you to read through this part of the lesson beforehand so you can begin thinking about your answers. There is a lot to cover in each lesson, so being somewhat familiar with the content before your meetings will save your group time when you actually do your study together.

Friendship Boosters. A big part of why you've come together is to deepen your friendships with other women and to support each other in meaningful ways. The questions and activities in this section are designed to link you together in bonds of friendship, faith, and joy. Whether you are meeting the other women in your group for the first time or are old friends, this section will boost the quality and pleasure in your relationships as well as give you opportunities to support each other in practical ways.

Just for Fun. God's plan for our lives certainly isn't all work and no play! Central to being a woman of faith is cultivating a joyful spirit, a balanced perspective, and an ability to enjoy life because of God's faithfulness and sovereignty. Every week you'll be given an idea or activity that will encourage you to enjoy your journey, laugh, and lighten your load as you travel the path toward wholehearted devotion together.

Praying Together. Nothing is more important than asking God to help you and your friends as you learn how to live out his truths in your lives. Each time you get together you'll want to spend some time talking to him about your individual and mutual concerns.

Making It Real in Your Own Life. You'll respond to these questions or activities on your own after group meetings, but don't consider them just an afterthought. This section is critical because it will help you discover more ways to apply what you've learned and discussed to your own life in the days and weeks ahead. This section will be a key to making God's liberating truths more real to you personally.

In each section, space is provided after each question for you to record your answers, as well as thoughts stimulated by others' answers during group discussion. While you can gain wisdom from completing parts of this guide on your own, you'll miss out on a lot of the power—and the fun!— of making it a group experience.

One woman should be designated as the group facilitator, but she needn't have any training in leading a Bible study or discussion group. The facilitator will just make sure the discussion stays on track, and there are specific notes to help her in the "Leader's Guide" section at the back of this book. Keeping your group size to between four and eight participants is ideal because then it will be possible for everyone to share each week. The length of time you'll need to complete the lessons together will depend largely on how much the participants talk, so the group facilitator will need to monitor the time to keep it under ninety minutes. The facilitator can also speed up or slow down the group time by choosing to skip some discussion questions or concentrate longer on others. If you decide to do this study in a larger group or Sunday school class, split up into smaller groups for discussion. Especially make sure no one gets left out of the process of building friendships and having fun!

Now that you've studied the map, your journey should go smoothly. Celebrate being women of faith as you travel together. *Enjoy!*

INTRODUCTION
A Part to Play

A story is told about a schoolboy who was trying out for a part in the school play. His mother knew he'd set his heart on it, but she was afraid he wouldn't be chosen. On the day the parts were assigned, she drove to school to pick him up. Her son rushed up to her, eyes shining with pride and excitement. Then he said some words to her that should remain a lesson to us all: "Oh Mom! I have been chosen to clap and cheer!"*

If only we could live life with this schoolboy's enthusiasm. The root of his excitement, of course, came from his deep trust in his director's choice of a role for him that she felt would fit the boy perfectly!

Our Master Director, Jesus Christ, has chosen parts for us to fulfill in the "play of life" that fit us perfectly as well. But often we, as the actors onstage or as a part of the behind-the-scenes crew, grumble and complain because we don't understand how vital our part is to the total performance. Whatever our role, the whole play would be lacking if we weren't doing what we were created to do.

In this guide to spiritual gifts, we'll be investigating God's grace bestowed on each of us (Eph. 4:7), given so we can fulfill our part in his divine drama. As varied as the actors and the backstage crew are the spiritual gifts God gives to us, his children. And our joyful journey would not be complete if we didn't take time to discover the interdependence and necessity of each drama participant as orchestrated by our Master Director.

---

*Illustrations for Biblical Preaching, edited by Michael P. Green (Grand Rapids: Baker, 1989), 352.

Every woman on her journey of faith is pursuing the answers to three great questions with which humankind has grappled since the beginning of time: *Who am I? Why am I here?* and *Where am I going?* This guide will help you find answers to the first two questions. As you discover and learn to use your own spiritual gifts, God will also grant you insight into why he has placed you here in life's drama in the first place.

With all of life's "to do" lists, household tasks, appointments, and stress, enjoy taking time to step back from the details to get a big-picture view of who you are and why God needs *you* as part of his "play."

Gifts Tagged "Uniquely You!"

Eternity magazine once told of a sidewalk flower vendor who was doing very little business. Suddenly, a happy thought struck him and he put up this sign: "Buy a gardenia! It will make you feel important all day long!" Almost immediately, his sales began to increase.

We all love to feel important, don't we? And buying a gardenia and wearing it perhaps can help a little in creating that feeling of significance. But God offers you a much greater sense of importance by giving you gifts with your name on them! As you unwrap and use each one, it will make you feel "uniquely you," different from others in God's family yet invaluable to them.

In this lesson, enjoy learning why God has chosen *your* gifts especially for you. Also discover how to guard against using them inappropriately while thriving on the unending blessings of utilizing them as God intended.

A Moment
for Quiet Reflection

1. How well do you know who God has made you? If your closest friends were to list your three greatest strengths, what do you think they would choose?

2. Think of a time recently when someone has enjoyed or benefited from one of your strengths. Did the person show appreciation? How did it make you feel? If you used one of your strengths anonymously, or your action went unnoticed, how did that make you feel?

> *Do not keep the alabaster boxes of your love and tenderness sealed up until your friends are dead. . . . Speak approving, cheering words . . . while their hearts can be thrilled and made happier by them.*
>
> GEORGE WILLIAM CHILDS

Knowing God's Heart

1. Read 1 Corinthians 12:4–6 together. What do all the gifts have in common? What makes them different?

2. What do you feel are the benefits of having these things in common with other gift recipients? of having things be different about the gifts each of us receives?

3. In the next three lessons we'll look more closely at the four lists of specific gifts the Bible mentions so you can discover whether you are a hand or a foot or even a gallbladder in the body of Christ! For now, read one of the lists in 1 Corinthians 12:7–13. How is each gift given? Why is each gift given?

4. How do you feel about God's reasons for giving his gifts?

5. What do these reasons tell us about God and how he wants to relate to us? about how he wants us to relate to one another?

6. Whenever we receive a gift, we can be tempted to use it unwisely. We can flaunt new clothes or recklessly drive a new car. We'll be happiest, however, when we use the gifts God gives in the way he designed us to use them. In verses 14–16 and 20–21, note what two types of statements we might be tempted to make as we discover our gifts.

7. With which of the above temptations do you struggle most frequently? Describe a time when you faced this temptation and what you did to try to overcome it.

8. Paul counters each of these temptations with God's perspective, which frees us to appreciate our—and everyone else's—unique part in the body. In 1 Corinthians 12:22–24 and 2 Corinthians 12:9–10, what hope does Paul offer when we are tempted to feel inferior?

9. What guidance does Paul give us for when we are tempted to feel superior? (See 1 Cor. 12:17–18 and Rom. 12:3, 10, 16.)

10. Share with your group a time when you felt inferior or superior. How could these truths in 1 Corinthians have helped you handle your situation and your feelings about yourself a little differently?

11. Read 1 Corinthians 12:18–19, 24–27. How does God arrange the parts of the body?

12. Why does he put us together the way he does?

13. Without naming names, who do you know right now who might fit into the category of feeling weaker or more dispensable to the body? What is one thing you could do to help that person receive greater honor?

14. Describe a time when you were suffering and what steps someone else took to suffer with you. Or when you were being honored and how someone went out of his or her way to rejoice with and honor you.

Friendship Boosters

1. Reread 1 Corinthians 12:26. As a group, identify which of the women among you are suffering right now. Which of you are being honored? Brainstorm ways you could obey Paul's instructions to suffer with those who are suffering and to rejoice with those who are being honored.

2. Choose the person on your right as the one you will rejoice or suffer with this week. Ask God to show you some small way you could let her know of your participation in her joy or sorrow, and take action in the week ahead.

Just for Fun

So you won't feel alone in your sorrows and joys, divide your group into two teams and take the following quiz before leaving. It will remind you of that "great cloud of [female] witnesses" (Heb. 12:1) who have gone on before you. Remember, they are watching and cheering you on from the grandstands even now! Try to complete the quiz without looking up the passages, but if you're stumped, feel free to consult your Bibles.

Match the following sorrow/joy with the correct woman of Scripture:

1. "Oh no! I'm having twins!"

   a. Rhoda (Acts 12:12–17)

2. "The waters are at flood level and it's still raining!"

   b. Abigail (1 Sam. 25)

3. "My mistress sent me away but God found me."

   c. Esther (Est. 4–8)

4. "I sure like fruit but eating it was a disaster for all of us!"

   d. Rebekah (Gen. 25:20–23)

5. "I lost a husband but gained a wonderful mother-in-law, a new land, and a new God."

   e. Hagar (Gen. 16)

6. "I arrived just in time to stop the anger of a king-in-waiting and eventually became his wife."

   f. Ruth (Ruth 1)

7. "Though I conceived out of wedlock, I carried the most precious child ever to be born."

   g. Eve (Gen. 3)

8. "Though my people were threatened with death, God gave us life due to my position."

   h. Mary (Luke 1–2)

9. "I was so frightened, I thought I had seen an angel. It was actually Peter whom God had released from prison!"

   i. Deborah (Judg. 4)

10. "I led the Israelites into battle when Barak wouldn't take the lead. God met us and we won!"

    j. Noah's wife (Gen. 6)

Praying Together

Spend a few minutes presenting each other to God, mentioning each woman's joy or sorrow. Ask God to help each of you honor those who need honoring and to suffer with those who need to feel your sorrow.

> *Friendship improves happiness, and abates misery,*
> *by doubling our joy, and dividing our grief.*
> JOSEPH ADDISON

Making It Real
in Your Own Life

1. Take some time to reflect on the three personal strengths you listed in the "Moment for Quiet Reflection" section. (We will begin to investigate in the next lesson the actual names of our spiritual gifts, but for now we will simply reflect on our strengths.) Now that you know that God gives spiritual gifts "for the common good," consider each of your strengths and how you have seen God use each one for the common good of his family. Write about a past situation when one of your strengths was used for the common good of others rather than just for yourself.

2. Write or say a prayer to God thanking him for each of the personal strengths you're aware of so far, and for his uniquely choosing to give you each one so you could bless others. Ask him to guard you from giving in to feelings of inferiority or superiority regarding each of your God-given abilities.

> *Lord Jesus, I am who I am by your loving design. Help me to accept my weaknesses as well as my strengths. Help me, too, to embrace myself in my totality as you embrace me, knowing I cannot do what was not ordained for me. May I contentedly serve you, love you, and luxuriate in what you empower me to do in your name and for your sake. Amen.*
>
> MARILYN MEBERG

Opening the Gifts— Part 1

Author Max DePree says it well: "A whale is as unique as a cactus. But don't ask a whale to survive Death Valley! We all have special gifts."

You're about to begin an adventure of discovery. Discovering how God has uniquely gifted you will help you decide whether you'll survive best, like the whale, in the Pacific Ocean or, like the cactus, in Death Valley! You are unique!

As the apostle Paul wrote to the churches of Rome, Corinth, and Ephesus, he described in general terms how he saw different individuals functioning in the body of Christ. Peter also, in his first letter, listed similar observations of the gifting of individuals. None of these four lists seems to be complete, although they are overlapping. Perhaps it was not Paul's intent to teach systematically about every possible spiritual gift, but simply to share general observations of how he saw the Spirit uniquely manifesting himself through the ministry and lives of individual believers.

There are many ways of categorizing spiritual gifts, although Scripture itself doesn't seem to classify them systematically. However, 1 Peter 4:10–11 does hint at two possible categories; and, for ease of discussion only, we will study the gifts with these categories in mind: *speaking gifts* and *serving gifts*.

Get ready to have fun learning who you are and how God has gifted you. You just might discover why you tend to thrive in the ocean rather than in the desert—or vice versa!

> *Each one should use whatever gift he has received to serve others, faithfully administering God's grace in its various forms. If anyone speaks, he should do it as one speaking the very words of God. If anyone serves, he should do it with the strength God provides, so that in all things God may be praised through Jesus Christ. To him be the glory and the power for ever and ever. Amen.*
>
> 1 PETER 4:10–11

A Moment for Quiet Reflection

When you think of relating to others in God's family, what do you love to do? Perhaps it's being with those who are hurting and need your listening skills. Perhaps it's organizing a committee or telephoning newcomers. As you consider what you tend to do "for the common good" of the body, complete the following statement:

In relating to God's family, I love to _____

_____.

> *My business is not to remake myself, but to make the absolute best of what God made.*
>
> ROBERT BROWNING

Knowing God's Heart

The four gift lists are found in the following passages: Romans 12:6–8; 1 Corinthians 12:8–11; Ephesians 4:11–13; and 1 Peter 4:9–11. If we were to divide these gifts into speaking gifts, serving gifts, and those which incorporate both speaking and serving, we might come up with the following lists:

Speaking Gifts	Speaking/Serving Gifts	Serving Gifts
prophecy (1 Cor. 14:1; Eph. 4:11; Rom. 12:6)	apostleship (Eph. 4:11)	helps/service (Rom. 12:7)
teaching (Rom. 12:7)	shepherding (Eph. 4:11)	hospitality (1 Peter 4:9)
evangelism (Eph. 4:11)	leadership (Rom. 12:8)	mercy (Rom. 12:8)
encouragement (Rom. 12:8)	administration (1 Cor. 12:28)	giving (Rom. 12:8)
discernment (1 Cor. 12:10)		healing (1 Cor. 12:9)
wisdom (1 Cor. 12:8)		miracles (1 Cor. 12:10)
knowledge (1 Cor. 12:8)		faith (1 Cor. 12:9)
tongues (1 Cor. 12:10)		intercession (not cited)
interpretation (1 Cor. 12:10)		creative ability (not cited)

Now that we have the big picture, let's investigate each individual gift. For each gift we'll suggest a definition if that Scripture does not give definitive ones. Some gifts with similar functions we'll look at together. We'll begin with the speaking gifts.

1. *Prophecy:* a God-given ability to declare truth with power and authority in such a way that edifies, strengthens, encourages, and comforts those who are listening.

   • Read 1 Corinthians 14:1–5. Why do you feel that Paul holds the gift of prophecy in such high regard as one of the "greater gifts" the church should "eagerly desire" or listen to whenever the church family gathers?

   • What might be the potential weaknesses of the prophet?

2. *Teaching:* a God-given ability to comprehend, clearly explain, and apply the Word of God to the lives of those listening.

   • Read James 3:1. Why do you suppose James says that those who teach will be judged more strictly?

   • Share with your group something you have learned recently because of another believer's teaching gift.

3. *Evangelism:* a God-given ability to communicate effectively the good news of salvation in Jesus Christ in such a way that nonbelievers respond in faith.

- Read John 4:28–29, 39–42. What evidence is there in these verses that the woman at the well immediately received the gift of evangelism as a result of her encounter with Christ?

- Do you feel anyone with the gift of evangelism was used by God to bring you to the Lord? If so, tell how God used that individual to move you one step closer to Christ or even into his eternal kingdom.

4. *Encouragement:* the God-given ability to affirm, build up, or reassure those who are discouraged, weakening in their faith, or need affirmation for their usefulness to others.

- Read Acts 9:26–27; 11:22–23. What was Barnabas's gift and how did he use it to benefit others?

5. *Wisdom:* the God-given ability to apply spiritual principles in a practical way that encourages listeners to identify steps that could be taken in a particular situation.

- Read 1 Kings 3:16–28. How did Solomon demonstrate his gift?

6. *Discernment:* the God-given ability to discern between truth and error, identifying deception or whether something is of God or not (also referred to as distinguishing between spirits).

- Read Acts 13:6–12. How did Paul demonstrate his gift? What evidence supports the fact that he used his gift correctly?

7. *Knowledge:* the God-given ability to acquire and communicate biblical and spiritual knowledge for the benefit of the church.

- Read Acts 8:26–38. How did Philip demonstrate his gift? What was the result?

8. Whom can you identify in God's family who perhaps possesses one of these four gifts (encouragement, wisdom, discernment, knowledge)? Share one specific recent incidence in which that person affected your life through the use of this particular gift.

9. *Tongues:* the God-given ability to speak in unintelligible languages in order to, through interpretation, edify the church.

- Read 1 Corinthians 14:2–5, 19. How does Paul describe the usefulness and the limitations of the gift of tongues?

10. *Interpretation of tongues:* the God-given ability to make known to the body of Christ the message of one who is speaking in tongues.

- Read 1 Corinthians 14:5, 26–28. What instructions does Paul give for the use of the gift of interpretation?

11. *Apostleship:* the God-given ability to be sent forth with a mission.

- Read 2 Corinthians 12:11–12; Acts 14:14; 1 Thessalonians 1:1; 2:6–7. What do you learn about the gift of apostleship from these passages, noting particularly individuals who possessed it?

- Apostles usually have a traveling ministry or a special ability to plant churches and oversee their development. Whom do you know or have you known in the larger body of Christ that has demonstrated this gifting? Why is this gift so important to the body of Christ?

12. *Shepherding or Pastoring:* the God-given ability to oversee, care for, and nurture individuals or a group in God's family and guide them toward maturity.

- Read Ephesians 4:11–12; 1 Peter 5:2–4. What character qualities will a gifted shepherd or pastor demonstrate?

13. *Leadership:* the God-given ability to inspire vision, and to motivate and direct a group of people to that vision resulting in the productive work of the ministry.

- Read 1 Thessalonians 5:12–13; Hebrew 13:7; Nehemiah 2:17–18; 2 Kings 12:6–8. From the passages given, list five characteristics of the gift of leadership.

14. *Administration:* the God-given ability to understand how an organization operates and facilitate the activities and procedures of others to increase the body's organizational effectiveness.

- Read 2 Kings 12:7–12. How is administration different from leadership?

- Will a good leader necessarily be a good administrator? Will a good administrator necessarily be a good leader? Why or why not?

- Which of the two gifts has a stronger emphasis on setting the goals in light of the vision? On devising and executing plans to carry out the goals?

15. Whom have you known in the body who has demonstrated one of these three gifts? Share the benefit you have received personally from one of the following:

- a shepherd: tell of a time when someone shepherded you through a challenging or discouraging situation

- a leader: describe the vision a leader set for your church and how you found a place of service within that overall vision

- an administrator: share how you personally benefited from someone else's organizational skills on behalf of God's family.

Friendship Boosters

At this point in your discovery, can you identify more readily with the speaking gifts or the serving gifts? (Remember, it is possible to have one or more gift(s) in each category.) Take turns answering this question and why you feel this way. Give each other feedback on your initial effort at classifying your gifts.

Just for Fun

1. Tear a sheet of paper into the shape of a body part which represents how you feel you function in God's family. If you love listening to the pain of others, perhaps you'll perceive yourself as the heart or the ear of the body. If you enjoy teaching others new truth, perhaps you'll perceive yourself as the brain. If you have unusual discernment or wisdom, perhaps you'll see yourself as the eye. (Since we haven't studied all the gifts yet, this exercise will only be an approximation of your gifts.) If you're uncertain as to which part of the body you are, ask for help! Often others perceive us better than we perceive ourselves.

2. Write your name on your claimed body part and work together to try to assemble the parts of the body into a whole person on the floor or on a table. (Caution: This could be funny!)

Praying Together

Hold hands around the "body" you've assembled and thank the Lord for each body part represented by the women in your group.

> *Lord, You know how much I long to work for You—*
> *For You have done so much within the heart of me.*
> *I must begin somewhere though talents may seem few*
> *Because about me there are needs I see.*
> *Perhaps I've been a bit too timid, Lord,*
> *Afraid to reach, to touch another life through mine.*
> *What joy that reaching, touching can afford*
> *When I join hands with Thee in work divine.*
> AUTHOR UNKNOWN

Making It Real
in Your Own Life

How are you feeling at this point about discovering that perhaps you are more the hands or feet of the body (service gifts) than the mouth (speaking gifts), or vice versa? Write to the Lord about your feelings and/or early impressions of your own giftedness. Then review the following verses: 1 Corinthians 12:7, 11, 14, 21, and 24. Let them reassure you that God knew just what he was doing when he gave you your part in his "play"!

Look to the horizon. Do you see the slightest change?
The slightest speck? If you do, follow it,
and God will reveal the rest.

HENRIETTA MEARS

Opening the Gifts— Part 2

One day Fanny Crosby, the well-known blind hymn writer, was desperately in need of a relatively small sum of money and had no idea where to get it. And so Fanny did what she normally would do: she began to pray. Moments later, there was a knock at the door and a stranger appeared with the exact amount of money she'd asked for! Fanny's heart burst forth immediately in a poem, later set to music and published as the hymn, "All the Way My Savior Leads Me."

Just think of it. One blind woman prays, and one God who isn't deaf hears and nudges one servant who *is* listening to knock on an unknown door. And one exuberantly grateful heart records a hymn we still enjoy today!

But that gift of song would never have been ours if it weren't for two obedient saints who invested their serving gifts for God's glory. Enjoy learning about these serving gifts, remembering Jesus' own words: "Whoever wants to become great among you must be your servant, and whoever wants to be first must become slave of all. For even the Son of Man did not come to be served, but to serve, and to give his life as a ransom for many" (Mark 10:43–45).

A Moment
for Quiet Reflection

1. Jesus came as a servant and served to the extent of giving
his life for us. Take a moment to *serve yourself* a cup of
tea, snuggle into your favorite easy chair, and reflect on all
the ways that Jesus served others while on the earth. Try
to make as extensive a list as possible. (If you need help,
check out the paragraph titles in the gospel of Mark, particularly chapters 1, 2, 5, 8, and 14. Check out John 13, too!)

2. Whom do you know who has modeled servanthood for
you? In what ways?

> *The Creator has made us each one of a kind.*
> *There is nobody else exactly like us, and there never*
> *will be. Each of us is his special creation and is alive*
> *for a distinctive purpose. Because of this, the person we*
> *are, and the contribution we make by being that very*
> *person, are vitally important to God. That makes me*
> *want to be today exactly who God made me, and*
> *no one else. This may be the last day I have.*
>
> LUCI SWINDOLL

Knowing God's Heart

1. *Hospitality:* the God-given ability to welcome and graciously care for and serve both strangers and guests through a receptive warm attitude and/or through the practical provisions of fellowship, food, and shelter. (Hospitality in Greek, the original New Testament language, means "to entertain strangers.")

   - Read Luke 10:38–42; Acts 18:24–26; 1 Corinthians 16:19; Hebrews 13:1–2; 1 Peter 4:9. According to these verses, what are some of the varied expressions of the gift of hospitality?

   - How has the use of this gift recently been modeled to you personally? What was done to help you feel "at home"? How could this modeling influence your approach when others come to visit you in your home, your church, or your place of employment?

2. *Mercy:* the God-given ability to empathize with those who are hurting and to minister cheerfully and appropriately to them in a way that helps ease their suffering.

- Read Mark 8:2–3; Romans 12:8; James 2:15–16. Again, this gift can take many forms. According to these verses, how can mercy be demonstrated?

- How have you demonstrated mercy to others? How has it been shown to you?

3. *Helps or Service:* the God-given ability to minister to others by completing practical and necessary tasks, thereby allowing others to succeed in their own area of giftedness (in the Greek, "to take a burden on oneself instead of leaving it on another").

- Read Acts 6:1–6; Philippians 2:25–30. How do these verses further clarify the roles of those with the gift of service.

- What differences do you see between the gifts of mercy and service?

- Tell of an instance when the "gift of mercy" was used to lift your spirit or soothe a personal wound. How did the person demonstrating this gift affect you?

- Share your appreciation for the gift of helps/service by completing the following sentence: (Name of person) enabled me to more fully succeed in ministry when he/she (practical task).

4. *Giving:* the God-given ability to contribute generously and cheerfully to the Lord's work through financial and material resources.

- Read 2 Corinthians 9:7–14. What does God do for the giver (vv. 6-9) ? What are God's responsibilities (vv. 10–11)?

- What appropriate attitudes accompany the gift of giving? How far-reaching are its results (2 Cor. 9:12–14)?

- Share a time when you were on the receiving end of someone's generous gift of giving. How did their gift impact your life? your spirit? your desire to give to others?

5. *Healing:* the God-given ability to be used as God's instrument to restore people to health.

- Read Acts 3:1–7; 5:15–16. Have you or has anyone you know been divinely healed? What was your response? What was the response of those close to you?

- Why do you think some people struggle with believing that God miraculously heals?

6. *Miracles:* the God-given ability to be used as God's instrument to appropriate an extraordinary amount of God's power in such a way that Christ is glorified and the message of the gospel is authenticated.

- Read Acts 2:43; 5:12–14.

- Have you ever seen one of these gifts, such as the gift of healing, functioning for the "common good" of the body? Do you feel that modern-day medical treatment and the gift of healing or the gift of miracles have any overlap? If so, explain how you have seen them work together for God's glory. If not, explain why not.

7. *Faith:* the God-given ability to trust that, in response to prayer, God will do what he says he is going to do.

- Read Acts 6:5–8; 11:24; 1 Corinthians 13:2; Hebrews 11:1. According to these verses, how can the body benefit from someone who has the gift of faith? What scriptural danger of the gift of faith is cited?

- When you were in a "stuck place," unable to believe God could work on your behalf, did you ever benefit from "riding on the coattails" of someone else's faith? If so, tell the group how that person's faith changed or freed you to believe God for the "impossible."

8. *Intercession:* the God-given ability to pray faithfully for others and to see God answer those prayers.

- Read Colossians 1:9–12; James 5:16. How have you seen the gift of intercession in action? How have you benefited from someone with this gift?

9. *Creative Ability:* the ability to advance God's work through creative skills such as drama, music, craftsmanship, graphic arts, painting, and so forth. (Though not listed on one of the four gift lists, read on for scriptural evidence of the Spirit's empowerment for these ministries.)

- Read Exodus 31:1–11; 2 Chronicles 5:12–14; 1 Samuel 16:23; 2 Samuel 23:1. What creative abilities were expressed through the Old Testament saints listed in the these passages?

- In the past year, how has your church family benefited from the creative gifts in the body? (Consider this: If God were to remove those gifts or hadn't given them in the first place, how would it affect your church family?)

Father, thank you that you designed me uniquely.
You gifted me uniquely, and you have a unique plan
for me. Show me that plan today, and give me the grace
and courage to live it out with gusto. Amen.
LUCI SWINDOLL

Friendship Boosters

1. This week you'll be completing the Spiritual Gifts Indicator located on page 81, which can help you pinpoint your own spiritual gifts. Draw names from a basket so you can check up on each other's progress later in the week regarding your completion of this Indicator.

2. In that you've focused today on the serving gifts, enjoy being servants to one another. Jesus performed the ultimate act of servanthood when he washed the disciples' feet. It even boosted their mutual friendships, for after the "foot-washing," Jesus called them his friends (John 13:5; 15:15)! Why not follow his example by washing each other's feet? All it takes is a towel and a basin and a servant's heart! Wash the feet of the woman to your right and allow the friend to your left to wash yours. If you feel more comfortable, wash one another's hands instead. As you serve one another, enjoy singing songs (or put on a cassette tape) about Jesus, your servant and friend.

Just for Fun

It's time for another matching quiz (on teams) with a prize for the winners! Which spiritual gift(s) do the following women of Scripture most likely possess? See how far you can get without referring to your Bible. (Hint: Those possessing two gifts are starred [*].)

1. Lydia (Acts 16:13–15)　　　　　a. leadership and prophecy

2. Priscilla　　　　　　　　　　　b. encouragement
   (Acts 18:24–26; 1 Cor. 16:19*)

3. Four daughters of Philip,　　　　c. hospitality
   the evangelist (Acts 21:9)

4. Dorcas (Tabitha) (Acts 9:36)　　d. prophecy

5. Joanna and Mary Magdalene   e. giving
   (Luke 8:1–3)

6. Phoebe (Rom. 16:1–2)   f. wisdom

7. Miriam (Ex. 15:20–21*)   g. giving

8. Deborah (Judg. 4:5*)   h. hospitality

9. Elizabeth (Luke 1:39–45)   i. leadership and prophecy

10. Mary, mother of Jesus   j. helps
    (Luke 1:38, 45; 2:19)

11. Woman at the Well   k. helps
    (John 4:28–29)

12. Martha (Luke 10:38)   l. evangelism

13. Hemorrhaging woman   m. faith
    (Mark 5:27–28, 34)

14. Abigail (1 Sam. 25,   n. faith
    particularly v. 33)

15. Poor widow (Mark 12:41–44)   o. teaching and hospitality

Praying Together

After everyone has been washed, thank God together for ways others have served you recently (e.g., an encouraging phone call, a note sent in the mail, a meal brought when you were sick, a prayer offered in faith). Begin your thank-you prayers focusing on group participants; then widen them to those outside the group.

We are pilgrims on a journey
We are sisters on the road
We are here to help each other
Walk the mile and share the load.

Sister, let me be your servant
Let me be as Christ to you
Pray that I might have the grace to
Let you be my servant too.

Making It Real
in Your Own Life

1. Capture a quiet moment to reflect on what you've discovered about your own spiritual gifts by filling out the Spiritual Gifts Indicator found on page 81. Begin in prayer, asking the Holy Spirit to reveal to you how he has uniquely gifted you to make an impact on others in the body. Don't forget to telephone the woman whose name you drew and ask for some feedback. Often others can discern our impact and therefore see our gifts better than we can ourselves.

2. If you feel you have identified your gifts or are within the ballpark, why not write a prayer to the Lord, thanking him for the gifts he has given you and asking for insight as to how you can use them for his glory. If you are still wondering, write an honest prayer of inquiry asking God how you could get further involved with his family so your gifts will be able to surface. Remember, if you are "in Christ," you *do* have a spiritual gift(s)!

> *All have a share in the beauty, all have a part in the plan.*
> *What does it matter what duty falls to the lot of a man?*
> *Someone has blended the plaster; someone has carried the stone;*
> *Neither the man nor the Master ever has builded alone;*
> *Make a roof for the weather, building a house for the King;*
> *Only by working together have men accomplished a thing.*
> AUTHOR UNKNOWN

Gifts for the Family

Christmas is a time for family. Songs like "I'll Be Home for Christmas" and "There's No Place Like Home for the Holidays" are favorites for many of us because they turn our hearts toward home. Though they aren't sung in honor of Mary and Joseph as they traveled to Joseph's hometown of Bethlehem for that first Christmas, they do remind us that God created the human family as a model of the kinds of relationships we're to have within his family.

One reason Christmas morning is so much fun for our family is because, as a pastor's family, we often receive family gifts given by other families in our church. Some of our favorites have been board games, fruit baskets, and tickets to a play or a special dinner out. One time we all received gift certificates to an unusual clothing store. What fun we had shopping together and then reporting to the family who gave the gift on our successful shopping spree!

God also loves giving "family gifts." As the best gift-giver ever, his family gifts are extravagant, given with great joy, and, when appreciated and used appropriately, benefit every member of the family. In this lesson, you'll discover what those family gifts are all about and how you, as God's family, can enjoy them to the fullest.

A Moment
for Quiet Reflection

1. Have you ever received a family or a group gift (e.g., your employer took the whole office on a trip or out to lunch, someone gave your family tickets to a show or baseball game, a neighbor gave an open house for all your neighbors)? If so, what was the gift?

2. What made the gift more enjoyable for you personally than if you had received the same gift individually?

Every good and perfect gift is from above,
coming down from the Father of the heavenly lights,
who does not change like shifting shadows.

JAMES 1:17

Knowing God's Heart

1. Tell the women in your group about your favorite group gift and what made it more enjoyable for you than if you had received it individually.

2. Read Ephesians 4:1–16 together. In verses 1–6, what suggestions does Paul give for living a life worthy of our calling?

3. Which of these is hardest for you? Why?

4. According to verse 3, the unity of the body takes effort. Discuss different ways you have seen others make an effort to keep or preserve the unity of the Spirit. Be as specific as you can.

5. Verses 7–10 tell us that grace has been given to each one of us. Grace here is defined as "a special endowment that brings responsibility for service." This grace, or our spiritual gifts, were "apportioned" or handed out by Christ after he "descended to earth" to pay for our sins. With Paul's reminder of our "slate being clean" and with our hearts challenged to unity, Paul goes on to remind us of the marvel of our diversity (vv. 11–15). We're united but different. When Christ gave out his grace, he wrapped it in a variety of packages. And some of those packages he gave as special gifts for all of us in his family to enjoy unwrapping. Though they are not our gifts per se, we get to enjoy and benefit from them. And we get to enjoy them together. According to verse 11, what are those special "family gifts"?

6. Why were the "family gifts" given to God's people (vv. 12–15)?

7. If the family of God were to refuse these family gifts, what would be forfeited as a result? In other words, what would the family look like or how would the family operate if these gifts weren't allowed to function?

8. How have you seen one or more of these "family gifts" used to bring about one of these purposes within your church or among the believers with whom you're intimately involved?

9. If possible, tell of a time in your experience with the body when one or more of these "family gifts" was squelched or was discouraged from functioning. What was the result?

10. According to verse 16, what part does Christ, the Head, play as these different gifts are in operation on behalf of the body?

11. We've already looked at the function of each of these family gifts. In the following examples, tell how each gift benefited the body of Christ.

- 1 Thessalonians 2:6–12: "Some to be apostles." Paul, Silas, and Timothy's benefit to the Thessalonian church:

- Acts 11:27–30; 21:10–11: "Some to be prophets." Agabus the prophet's benefit to the Judean Christians, to Paul, and to the Jerusalem believers:

- Acts 8:4–5, 26–40: "Some to be evangelists." Philip the evangelist's (Acts 21:8) benefit to Samaria, to Ethiopia, and beyond:

- Philippians 2:19–23: "Some to be pastors." Timothy's benefit to the Philippian church:

- Acts 20:25–27: "Some to be teachers." Paul's benefit to the Ephesian church:

12. Take turns sharing how each of you individually have benefited from one or more of these "family gifts." Whom do
you know who has one or more of these gifts and who has
used them to build up the body of Christ?

13. Read Hebrews 13:7, 17. In that these "family gifts" benefit
those of us in the family, what specific ways are we to
encourage those with these "family gifts" in their ministry
to us? How do you feel they would benefit from these
encouragements?

Friendship Boosters

Exchange names with the woman whose family size is
closest to yours. Find a way this week to bless her family. Maybe
you can prepare a favorite dessert. Perhaps an offer to baby-sit for
an evening would be welcome. Maybe you could take a fun family
photo for them. Don't feel compelled to spend a lot of money, just
think together of ways you could bless each other's families!

Just for Fun

As a group, brainstorm a creative, even zany, way you could bless someone among the believers with whom you have been involved who has one of these "family gifts." If there is someone you all know and have been blessed by, choose them as your common "love project." (If you all aren't from the same church or Christian organization, you may need to team up in 2s or 3s to complete this assignment.) The sky's the limit. Helium balloons at his or her desk, singing telephone calls, cookies or cakes for his or her family are just a few possibilities. Have fun with this as you love them lavishly and perhaps a little outrageously! They need to laugh and enjoy life, too, and benefit from knowing of your love and appreciation.

> *I shall pass this way but once; any good, therefore, that I can do or any kindness that I can show to any human being, let me do it now. Let me not defer nor neglect it, for I shall not pass this way again.*
> STEPHEN GRELLET

Praying Together

Spend some time thanking God for each other and the spiritual gifts God has given you. You could even begin with simple sentence prayers of "Thank you, God, for (woman's name) who has the gift of _____." Then thank God for those who have ministered to you with one of these "family gifts." Again, sentence prayers can be helpful:

"Thank you, God, for (person's name) who has the 'family gift' of _____ who has ministered to me by _____."

Ask God to show you ways you can support and encourage those with "family gifts" in their ministry to you and to others.

Making It Real in Your Own Life

Perhaps an individual possessing one of these "family gifts" has been particularly influential in your own life. He or she has built you up in Christ and helped you grow more than any other individual. When Jesus healed the ten lepers, only one came back and said thank you. Perhaps this parable is representative of how few of us say thank you to those who minister to us. Why not be a "ten percenter" and write a letter expressing your personal thanks for this individual's ministry in your life. If the person is no longer living, you could still write a letter, poem, or tribute to them and share it with your group next week.

> *Who is the happiest of men? He who values*
> *the merits of others, and in their pleasure takes joy,*
> *even as though it were his own.*
> GOETHE

Pleasing the Gift-Giver

*T*ake my life and let it be consecrated, Lord, to Thee."

The poet who penned these words, Frances Ridley Havergal, was a living testimony to her own poetry. The line, "Take my voice and let me sing," was written by one considered to be a naturally gifted musician. Frances trained as a concert soloist and was well known for her "unusually pleasing voice." Her musical talents could probably have brought her much fame and fortune. Instead, she was determined to dedicate herself to sing and work for Jesus alone.

The line, "Take my silver and my gold," was also a living reality for her. At one point, Frances gathered all her finest jewelry and family heirlooms and shipped them to the church missionary house to be used for evangelizing the lost.

Frances is one who pleased the Gift-Giver in the way she implemented her talents. In this lesson you'll discover how to please the Gift-Giver by properly implementing your spiritual gifts while avoiding improper use of them. Take a moment to pray as Frances Havergal did:

> Take my love, my God, I pour;
> at Thy feet its treasure store.
> Take myself and I will be
> ever only all for Thee; ever only all for Thee.

I'll go where you want me to go, dear Lord,
real service is what I desire.
I'll sing a solo any time, dear Lord,
but don't ask me to sing in the choir.

I'll do what you want me to do, dear Lord,
I like to see things come to pass.
But don't ask me to teach boys and girls, O Lord,
I'd rather just stay in my class.

I'll do what you want me to do, dear Lord,
I yearn for Thy kingdom to thrive.
I'll give you my nickels and dimes, dear Lord,
but please don't ask me to tithe.

AUTHOR UNKNOWN

A Moment
for Quiet Reflection

1. Have you ever given a gift to someone who used it recklessly, carelessly, or destructively? Can you remember giving a gift to someone who loved it and used it as you hoped they would? How did either or both make you feel?

2. What might bring pleasure to God's heart as you use his gifts to you? What might you anticipate would hurt him as you use the gifts he's given?

Knowing God's Heart

What a privilege to please the Gift-Giver. As we use our spiritual gifts properly, we'll hear him say, "Well done, good and faithful servant." Let's look at three ways we can please him.

1. We can please God, the Gift-Giver, by submitting to the Holy Spirit.

   - Read John 15:5; Ephesians 5:18; Acts 4:31. What do these verses teach about submitting to the Holy Spirit as we use our gifts?

   - Tell of a time when you really felt the Holy Spirit filling you and working through you as you used your gifts. What might have happened if you had not submitted to the Holy Spirit's leadership and filling?

2. We can please God by appropriately using our own personal gift mix. Most of us will have more than one spiritual gift. Appropriate use of my gift mix can be defined as "the effective working together of my spiritual gifts for God's glory." For instance, someone might have the gifts of wisdom, hospitality, and mercy. Her gift mix might work together best by her opening her home to an unwed mother, showing mercy and imparting wisdom as she helps that mother cope with an unwanted pregnancy.

   Someone else might have the gift of wisdom, but her gift mix is comprised of teaching, wisdom, and administration.

Her gift mix might best be used through teaching a large Sunday school class, overseeing its administration, and handling some of its personal counseling. Both individuals have gifts of wisdom, but each will use that gift differently according to her own gift mix.

Our gift mix will often determine where we will function best in the body. Understanding our gift mix may help two individuals with one or two overlapping gifts to appreciate their similarities while freeing one another to appropriate their gifts differently.

- What might have been the gift mix of the following people of Scripture?

  Priscilla: (Acts 18:24–26; 1 Cor. 16:19)

  Silas: (Acts 15:22, 30–32; 1 Thess. 1:1; 2:6)

- As well as you currently can determine, what is your own personal gift mix?

- How might your gift mix determine where and/or how you might function in the body of Christ or in your church family? Share this with your group.

3. We can please God by appreciating ministry-team gift blends. If each individual has a gift mix, then ministry teams will need to appreciate and appropriate the gift mixes of each team member in order to discover the ministry team's gift blend. Let's investigate a scriptural example.

- Paul, Silas, and Timothy were a ministry team on Paul's second missionary journey. What might have been their individual gift mixes?

  Silas: (Acts 15:22, 30–32; 1 Thess. 1:1; 2:6)

  Paul: (1 Tim. 2:7; Acts 15:35; 16:6–10)

  Timothy: (1 Tim. 4:11–16; 1 Thess. 1:1; 2:6; Phil. 2:19–20)

- How might their individual gift mixes have worked together as a gift blend? for greater effectiveness for Christ's kingdom?

- On what ministry teams have you functioned in the past or are you presently functioning (i.e., Sunday school class ministry team, a home Bible study, or a church committee)? Focus on one, writing down the names of team members and what you perceive might be the spiritual gifts of each. How did those gift mixes function as a gift blend? Feel free to learn from the examples of others if you have not yet functioned as part of a ministry team.

We can also please the Gift-Giver by resisting the improper use of our spiritual gifts. Let's look at three things we need to resist in order to avoid improper use of our gifts.

4. *Resist pride.*

- Read Ezekiel 28:12, 14, 17. Why did God throw Satan out of heaven? How does your answer cast light on the commands Peter gives us in 1 Peter 5:5–9?

- Tell of a situation when pride in your gifts and/or talents was a temptation for you. Did you resist? If not, how could you have resisted?

5. *Resist jealousy.*

- How does 1 Corinthians 3:1–6 encourage us to resist jealousy?

- Why is jealousy such a destructive disease to develop?

- Is there a particular spiritual gift you don't possess of which you can tend to be jealous? Do you have any insight as to why that particular gift is a stumbling block to you? If you're stumped, perhaps your group can help you answer this question.

6. *Resist gift glorification* (one disease with three strains).

- How do the following Scripture passages encourage us to resist the three strains of the disease of gift glorification?

  Strain #1: exalting one gift above another (1 Cor. 12:21–23)

Strain #2: leading with gifts rather than the fruit of the Spirit (Gal. 5:22–23; 1 Cor. 13:1–3)

Strain #3: loving the gifts above the Giver (Acts 8:13, 18–24; Col. 3:23–24)

- Gift glorification is a form of idol worship. Whenever we love something or someone more than Christ, it becomes an idol and we become idol worshipers. What has worked for you in keeping you from exalting:

  your gifts above the gifts of others?

  your gifts above the Spirit's fruit?

  your gifts above the Giver?

7. To which misuse of gifts are you most prone to give in: pride, jealousy, or gift glorification (which strain)? Complete on a 3 x 5 card the statement below, filling in the blank with your greatest temptation.

Lord, help (your name) to resist (pride, jealousy, gift glorification, strain 1, 2, or 3).

Friendship Boosters

1. Consider your own gift blend as a group. How have you seen your gift blend in operation as you have been together for this study?

2. Perhaps there is a ministry to which God might call some of you together resulting from your growing comfort level with your gift blend. Discuss this possibility, while keeping in mind other ministries to which God has perhaps already called each of you. Or perhaps one or two of you will feel led to join others from your group in a ministry in which she is or they are already serving, adding your gift mix to their ministry team's gift blend. Let the Spirit lead you as you discuss how your gift blend(s) can be used for the glory of God.

Just for Fun

Draw names from a "hat." This week buy a five-dollar gift for the individual whose name you drew. Look carefully for a gift you feel is appropriate for that individual, keeping in mind what you've learned about her from this study. Wrap and bring the gift with you next week.

Praying Together

1. Pray that each group member would know where she is to fit on a ministry team and how her gift mix can enhance a team's gift blend.

2. Pass your cards to the person on your left, and pray for each other simply by reading out loud the completed statement you received. Leave a moment of silence after reading each statement so women can pray silently for each individual. If all in the group feel comfortable, these silent prayers could even be spoken out loud.

Making It Real
in Your Own Life

Write a prayer to the Lord, letting him know of your desire to please only him as the Gift-Giver. Ask him to help you resist any improper use of your gifts, and tell him of your desire to properly use your gifts, implementing principles this lesson has taught you.

Be honest with him. This may lead to a time of confession for improper use of your gifts, a time of thanksgiving for how he has used you in the past or is presently using you, or even a time of supplication as you ask him to place you where your gift mix could be used to the fullest.

If he is choosing not to use you right now, perhaps his desire is to refine your character for future ministry. If you feel this might be true, ask him for wisdom as to how to participate willingly in his refining process.

God develops character to match His assignments.
If you can't be faithful in a little, God will
not give you a larger assignment.
HENRY T. BLACKABY AND CLAUDE V. KING

Unopened Gifts

When I was growing up, Christmas morning was a time for opening presents as a family. Later that day we'd spend time celebrating with my aunt and uncle. They loved us lavishly, especially since they had no children of their own. And it showed in the kind of gifts they gave us.

I can remember one Christmas in particular, when I really wanted a Brownie dress because I had just joined a Brownie troop. I unwrapped package after package, but no Brownie dress emerged. Still, there were presents under my aunt's tree, and I was just sure the one tagged for me would be my long-awaited Brownie dress.

As my brother handed out the gifts, I didn't even mind being the last to receive mine. I imagined it was all a part of the suspense. My fingers fumbled and my heart pounded as I untied the bow and ripped into the paper of the box just the right size and shape for a Brownie dress. As I pulled back the tissue paper, however, I burst into tears. The dress before me wasn't brown at all, but instead a light blue delicate eyelet. It didn't matter how beautiful it was; it wasn't what I had longed for. And with no more presents under the tree my hope was exhausted. As I sat there in my puddle of tears, my aunt sauntered into the next room and brought out one more unwrapped gift. And, of course, inside was my treasured Brownie dress.

Now reverse the story for a moment. Imagine my aunt's anticipation at giving me the Brownie dress. What if instead of excitedly ripping into the package I had merely ignored it? She may have been the one to burst into tears instead of me. Maybe that's how God feels when we leave his gifts unopened. He knows that we are missing out on his best for us. Unwrap the gifts he gives you and experience the extravagant joy that comes from using them for his glory. Now take a look at the parable of the talents. Allow it to motivate you not to leave any of God's gifts tagged for you unopened and unused.

A Moment
for Quiet Reflection

1. Can you remember a time you really wanted a gift but didn't receive it? Take a moment to reflect on how you felt at the time.

2. As we approach the close of our study on spiritual gifts, do you feel you have any God-given spiritual gifts that you aren't presently using? Why do you suppose you have been leaving that gift unwrapped and still in the box? If you are not sure why, perhaps our study will give you further insight.

> *Only one life, 'twill soon be past.*
> *Only what's done for Christ will last.*
> AUTHOR UNKNOWN

Knowing God's Heart

1. Read Matthew 25:14–30. How did the man going on a journey decide to take care of his assets? What specific actions
did he take (vv. 14–15)?

2. What did each servant do with what the Master entrusted
to him (vv. 16–18)? How do their choices give insight into
our options for what we do with our talents/spiritual gifts?

3. Verse 19 tells us the Master stayed away a long time before
returning to settle accounts. What might that reveal about
the Master (2 Peter 3:8–9 may help)?

4. How did the Master respond to the man with five talents? With two talents (vv. 21–23)? What did each of the Master's responses to the first two servants reveal about his character and heart?

5. What do the Master's responses teach us about how God responds to our investment of talents and/or spiritual gifts?

6. As a result of your investment of one of your spiritual gifts, how have you heard God say to you recently, "Well done, good and faithful servant"? Share this experience with your group.

7. Whom do you know who has been a good and faithful servant? How have you seen that person "share in the Master's happiness"?

8. How did the third servant perceive the Master? Do you feel his perception was accurate? Why or why not? Did the Master agree with the servant's perception of him (vv. 24–27)? Try to support your answer from the text.

9. Tell of a time your perception of the Master was less than accurate (or perhaps it's inaccurate right now). Why did you (or do you) perceive him the way you did (do)? What brought about (or could bring about) your changed view?

10. In that this story is meant to be a parable teaching us lessons about life, what "lessons for life" do you glean from it, particularly related to the use of your spiritual gifts?

11. What tempted each of the following people to want to bury their talent?

(Temptation to bury your talent = that which tempts you to disobey God.)

Match the following. Perhaps each participant could look up a different Scripture passage or feel free to answer from memory.

1. Third servant (Matt. 25:26)

    a. not as qualified as someone else

2. Ananias and Sapphira (Acts 5:1–10)

    b. jealousy

3. Gideon (Judg. 6:36–40)

    c. too young

4. Jeremiah (Jer. 1:4–10) and Timothy (1 Tim. 4:12)

    d. laziness

5. Ten spies (Num. 13:26-33)

    e. wanted proof first of God's ability to work through him

6. King Saul (1 Sam. 18:5–9)

    f. too busy with business and family

7. Moses (Ex. 4:10–13)

    g. greed

8. Invited guests (Luke 14:15–21)

    h. fear; perceived enemy as bigger than themselves

12. With which of the above temptations can you most easily identify? Which one most frequently causes *you* to want to bury your talent?

> *Whoever sows sparingly will also reap sparingly, and whoever sows generously will also reap generously.*
>
> 2 CORINTHIANS 9:6

Friendship Boosters

1. On a slip of paper, have each woman answer the following:

What spiritual gift do you most frequently tend to bury?

What temptation (see #11) most frequently tempts you to bury this talent or leave it as an unwrapped gift in the box?

What simple way could a friend help or encourage you to unwrap this gift more regularly and use it for God's glory?

2. Put the slips of paper in a basket facedown and have each woman draw out one. If you all feel comfortable, read the slips out loud identifying its owner. Ask God to help you fulfill the simple request your friend has made of you.

> *Please note Jesus doesn't say, "Because you have been successful in a very small matter." He says, "Because you have been trustworthy." God is not scrutinizing the success of your marriage or the results of your mission.... Every Christian is on the same playing field. Success isn't the key. Faithfulness is. Being bigger and better is not the point. It's being obedient.*
>
> JONI EARECKSON TADA

Just for Fun

Last week you drew names to buy five-dollar gifts for each other. It's important not to leave them unopened in the box! Have fun opening your gifts, while each gift-giver explains why she chose this particular gift for her friend.

Praying Together

Take the information from these slips to prayer, asking God to help each of you to use the gifts he has given. Ask him to enable you to be continual encouragers of one another to use your gifts.

Making It Real
in Your Own Life

Write a prayer to God thanking him for this study, for the greater understanding of how he has created you and wants to use you for the greater good of the growth of his family. If there is a gift or gifts you haven't been using or haven't had the opportunity to use yet, ask him to be the one to open the door for you so you might use that gift for his glory.

Love through me, love of God,
Make me like Thy clear air
Through which unhindered, colors pass
As though it were not there.

Powers of the love of God,
Depths of the heart Divine,
O Love that faileth not, break forth,
And flood this world of Thine.

AMY CARMICHAEL

SPIRITUAL GIFTS INDICATOR

The Spiritual Gifts Indicator works like a chronological funnel, with each step of the process leading to the next step, narrowing down your possibilities. You may want to take ten minutes alone to answer questions on yourself prior to group discussion.

In Christ
Involvement
Interests
Impact on Others
Increased Joy

Hint:
When you give your life to Jesus, the Holy Spirit comes to live inside you. He brings with him his spiritual gifts. If you are not "in Christ" yet, though you may have natural talents, you do not have any gifts of the Spirit (1 Corinthians 12:3, 11). Perhaps you would like to consider right now giving your life to Christ. Ask someone in your group to help you take this all-important first step.

IN CHRIST

Are you "in Christ" or on the way?

❏ in Christ
❏ on the way

Hint:
In that our spiritual gifts are given for the common good of the body, we cannot discover our gifts in isolation. If you are not presently involved anywhere in God's family, your first step toward discovering your spiritual gifts will be to get involved! Consistent exposure to others will enable your gifts to begin to surface.

INVOLVEMENT

Are you involving yourself with the body of Christ? Where and how are you presently involved (i.e., Bible study participant, church attendance, on a committee)? List below your areas of involvement:

_____

_____

_____

_____

INTERESTS

Hint:

As you get involved in God's family, certain areas of interest will begin to surface over time that will point you toward your spiritual gifts. Spiritual gifts surface with maturity. If you are a fairly new Christian, it will be harder to recognize your spiritual gifts or even your areas of interest. Just keep loving Jesus and his family and your gifts will become apparent. The questions to the left will begin to help you pinpoint your areas of interest.

Do your interests lie more in:

❑ speaking gifts or
❑ serving gifts (review list on page 27)
❑ people
❑ tasks
❑ content
❑ building believers in Christ
❑ introducing unbelievers to Christ

Do you feel more drawn to:

❑ children
❑ adults
❑ teens
❑ couples
❑ singles/young adults
❑ elderly
❑ those with special needs
❑ _____

Do you prefer:

❑ one-on-one ministry
❑ small-group ministry
❑ large-group ministry
❑ behind-the-scenes ministry

IMPACT ON OTHERS

Hint:

In that the gifts are given for the common good of the body, perhaps the best way of determining your spiritual gifts is by sensing your impact on others. Something may be an area of interest, but if you are not making impact for the common good when you are functioning in that capacity, probably it is not a spiritual gift. Answering the questions to the right may help clarify your impact.

Most likely, your group will be able to help define your impact even better than you can.

When people affirm you for the impact you are making in their lives, in what areas do the affirmations tend to cluster?

1. _____

2. _____

3. _____

To confirm these areas as spiritual gifts, ask yourself questions similar to the following:

If you think
your gift is ... Ask

Teaching ... Are people learning?

Hospitality ... Do people feel at home?

Intercession ... Do others find God moving in their lives in answer to your prayers?

Leadership ... Do others look to you for leadership and vision and feel led to follow your direction?

Administration ... Do others feel more organized when you are around?

Helps ... Do others feel helped in the use of their gifts by ways you feel led to step in and give them assistance?

Mercy ... Do others feel heard and sympathized with when they talk with you?

Add your own pertinent questions below:

_____

_____

_____

_____

_____

_____

_____

_____

When you are function-
ing effectively in an area
of giftedness, you will
experience a sense of
increased joy from being
used by the Holy Spirit
in the life or lives of
others. If you are also
impacting them for their
good, you are function-
ing in an area of your
giftedness.

INCREASED JOY

When have you felt great joy from being used
in the life or lives of others? What were you doing?

_____

_____

_____

_____

_____

_____

_____

_____

LEADER'S GUIDE

LESSON ONE

General background on the church at Corinth: The church at Corinth was a very spiritually gifted church, "not lacking any spiritual gift" (1 Cor. 1:7). Its extreme giftedness, however, made its members vulnerable to pride and strong opinions leading to divisions on many topics—i.e., on favorite teachers (Paul or Apollos—ch. 3), on taking legal action even against fellow believers (ch. 6), on varying views of marital purity (ch. 7). Therefore it's not surprising that the Corinthian church was conflicted and divided in its view of spiritual gifts as well, elevating one gift above another. Paul counters this type of distorted thinking with an analogy of the parts of the body all needing and being of equal importance to all the other parts, emphasizing that each is needed for the "common good" of the body not for selfish or divisive gain.

6. The two types of statements are:

Because I am not _____ I do not belong to the body. ("I am not as important as someone else.")

Because I am _____ I have no need of the rest of the body. ("I don't need anyone else.")

The first statement speaks of yielding to a temptation to inferior feelings due to a false self-perception of being given inferior gifts when no such gifts exist from God's perspective.

The second statement speaks of yielding to a temptation to superior feelings due to an inflated false perception of possessing superior gifts when, again, from God's perspective, no such gifts exist or are given to the body's members.

Just for Fun. Key to Matching Quiz

1. *d*
2. *j*
3. *e*
4. *g*
5. *f*
6. *b*
7. *h*
8. *c*
9. *a*
10. *i*

LESSON TWO

As you prepare to read the Scripture out loud as a group, it might be helpful if the women look up the references for each of the four gift lists. (You might have the women pair up, depending on the number of participants.) Have a basket of small strips of paper on hand so passages can be marked and turned to more easily.

1. The church at Corinth, not individuals within the church, was encouraged corporately to seek the "greater gifts," exposing them to the entire body when gathered. Personally, we cannot seek after specific spiritual gifts because they are given by the "Spirit just as he determines" (1 Cor. 12:11).

2. Because a teacher has the potential of having great influence over her students, she will be held more accountable for what she teaches. Because she spends so much time preparing, she also will know more and therefore be expected to apply more to her own personal life, modeling to her students what she teaches.

13. Use the 2 Kings passages to help clarify the difference between the gift of leadership (King Joash) and administration (Jehoiada and the priests).

   Gift Lists. Intercession/Creative Ability (not cited). The serving gifts of intercession and creative ability are not cited on any of the four gift lists but are often considered as spiritual gifts. For reasons why, see Leader's Notes in Lesson 3, question 8.

   Just for Fun. Provide one piece of plain white paper per woman with which she can create her body part. A black marker could also be made available so women can boldly mark their paper with the particular body part with which they can most readily identify.

LESSON THREE

Again, it might be helpful to have each woman (or pair/team of women) look up the related Scriptures prior to reading them aloud. As with the previous lesson, small strips of paper could be used as markers so passages can be turned to more easily.

2 & 3. The difference between the gift of mercy and the gift of helps: those with the gift of mercy receive blessing from aiding those who are suffering while those with the gift of helps receive blessing from aiding those ministering to others.

4. The far-reaching results of giving include a deep gratitude and a love in the hearts of the recipients for the givers, moving them to thank God and to pray for those who have given to them.

8. If Paul's lists of gifts were not meant to be all-inclusive, then intercession could be considered as a spiritual gift in that we readily can recog-

nize its function within the church today. It seems that God has gifted some within his family to love to pray on behalf of others and to find great joy, satisfaction, and success from their times of intercession.

Friendship Boosters. Have necessary supplies for foot- or hand-washing: a basin, washcloth, soap, towel, and perhaps even some scented lotion. Be prepared with hymns or choruses to sing, or bring along a praise and worship cassette and player.

Just for Fun. Key to Matching Quiz

1. *c* or *h*
2. *o*
3. *d*
4. *j* or *k*
5. *e* or *g*
6. *j* or *k*
7. *a* or *i*
8. *a* or *i*
9. *b*
10. *m* or *n*
11. *l*
12. *c* or *h*
13. *m* or *n*
14. *f*
15. *c* or *g*

Making It Real in Your Own Life. The Spiritual Gifts Indicator is given here to enable participants to help discover their gifts. It is given in lieu of a comprehensive spiritual gifts inventory or test which is beyond the capacity of this study guide to provide. If your group would like to take such a test, I would recommend *Discover Your Gifts Workbook* (Grand Rapids, Church Development Resources, 1983).

LESSON FOUR

4. Paul puts a strong emphasis in v. 3 on everyone making an effort to keep the unity of the Body. When the "family gifts" are allowed to function, Paul reemphasizes that one of the outcomes will be the unity of the body (v. 13).

11. As a time-saver, perhaps each participant could locate a different Scripture and be prepared to read or summarize what she learns.

Agabus was used of the Lord, as prophets often are, to bring clarity and truth in the midst of confusion (a mark of the evil one). Compare Acts 20:22; 21:4; and 21:10–14 to see how Agabus spoke truth to Paul's spirit to help eliminate the confusion created by those trying to keep him from going to Jerusalem.

LESSON FIVE

1. The statement, "Be filled with the Spirit," is in the present tense and is best translated as "keep on being filled." The verb is also passive. We cannot fill ourselves but we can give the Spirit permission to fill us.

3. Probable gift mixes of Paul's second missionary team include:

    Silas's gift mix: leadership, prophecy, encouragement, apostleship
    Paul's gift mix: apostleship, teaching, leadership
    Timothy's gift mix: teaching, apostleship, pastor

    All three were gifted and called as apostles to plant churches. Both Silas and Paul were gifted in leadership and vision which would have enabled the team to hear clearly the Holy Spirit's "big picture" for their journey. Silas's gifting as a prophet and an encourager would have added great personal insight to the team for effective ministry to individuals. Coupled with Timothy's pastor's heart for each sheep in God's flock, the team was well-equipped to minister on the personal level to all they met. Paul's gift of teaching would have been most necessary as they traveled from city to city bringing many new converts to Christ who needed to be taught the basics. In addition, Paul must have seen Timothy as a teacher in training during this journey as he later encouraged Timothy to use his gift of teaching and not have anyone look down on him because he was young.

4. Pride is the devil's trademark and is what originally caused God to throw the devil out of heaven. When we grow proud of what only the Spirit can do through us, we are no longer under God's mighty protecting hand. Removed from his protection, we become a prime target for the prowling lion looking for someone to devour. Pride is a dangerous sin because we end up snatching God's glory for what only he can do through us. Our spiritual gifts are from him, the empowerment for their use is from his Spirit, and he must get all the glory for what he does through us.

7. Provide index cards for the group.

    Just for Fun. Provide a "hat" and name slips.

LESSON SIX

5. The Master had the same response to each of the first two servants. We are held accountable for and rewarded according to how we invest what God has given us, not for what we haven't been given.

8. The third servant was wicked because he deliberately tried to make himself look good and his master look bad. He distorted the truth when he said, "Look, you have what is yours," because he actually owed his master not only one talent, but also whatever it would have earned had he

invested it. But instead of acknowledging his shortcomings, he acted as if the Master should have rewarded him for being cautious and for having returned the entire talent unaltered. This statement reveals the hidden agenda of his heart and confirms that the Master's perception of him was accurate. He was indeed wicked and lazy.

11. Key

1. *d*
2. *g*
3. *e*
4. *c*
5. *h*
6. *b*
7. *a*
8. *f*

Friendship Boosters. Provide "basket" and slips of paper.

Look for these faith-building resources from Women of Faith:

Friends Through Thick & Thin by Gloria Gaither, Peggy Benson, Sue Buchanan, and Joy Mackenzie
    Hardcover 0-310-21726-1

We Brake for Joy! by Patsy Clairmont, Barbara Johnson, Marilyn Meberg, Luci Swindoll, Sheila Walsh, and Thelma Wells
    Hardcover 0-310-22042-4

Bring Back the Joy by Sheila Walsh
    Hardcover 0-310-22023-8
    Audio Pages 0-310-22222-2

The Joyful Journey by Patsy Clairmont, Barbara Johnson, Marilyn Meberg, and Luci Swindoll
    Softcover 0-310-22155-2
    Audio Pages 0-310-21454-8

Joy Breaks by Patsy Clairmont, Barbara Johnson, Marilyn Meberg, and Luci Swindoll
    Hardcover 0-310-21345-2

Women of Faith Journal
    Journal 0-310-97634-0

Promises of Joy for Women of Faith
    Gift Book 0-310-97389-9

Words of Wisdom for a Woman of Faith
    Gift Book 0-310-97390-2

Prayers for a Woman of Faith
    Gift Book 0-310-97336-8

We want to hear from you. Please send your comments about this book
to us in care of the address below. Thank you.

ZondervanPublishingHouse
Grand Rapids, Michigan 49530
http://www.zondervan.com